**Redleaf** *Quick* Guide

Behavioral Challenges in Early Childhood Settings

REVISED EDITION

Connie Jo Smith, EdD

Redleaf Press®
www.redleafpress.org
800-423-8309

Published by Redleaf Press
10 Yorkton Court
St. Paul, MN 55117
www.redleafpress.org

First edition published 2008. Second edition 2017.
Cover design by Jim Handrigan
Cover photo by iStock.com/Inara Prvsakova
Typesetting by Douglas Schmitz
Typeset in Signo and Avenir
Printed in the United States of America

Library of Congress Cataloging-in-Publication Data

Names: Smith, Connie Jo, author.
Title: Behavioral challenges in early childhood settings / Connie Jo Smith,
   Connie Jo Smith, EdD.
Description: Revised Edition. | St. Paul, MN : Redleaf Press, 2017.
Identifiers: LCCN 2017000152 (print) | LCCN 2017019995 (ebook) | ISBN
   9781605545257 (ebook) | ISBN 9781605545240 (paperback)
Subjects: LCSH: Behavior modification. | Early childhood education. |
   Classroom management. | BISAC: EDUCATION / Preschool & Kindergarten. |
   EDUCATION / Reference. | EDUCATION / Classroom Management.
Classification: LCC LB1060.2 (ebook) | LCC LB1060.2 .S589 2017 (print) | DDC
   371.39/3--dc23
LC record available at https://lccn.loc.gov/2017000152

Printed on acid-free paper   U23-03

This book is dedicated to my mother, Nevolyn C. Smith, for the many times I have behaved in challenging ways. And to Breanne Thompson Perry, who made my life richer by providing me with firsthand experience in facing challenging behaviors of children at home.

CONTENTS

ACKNOWLEDGMENTS

True appreciation is expressed to Kara Lomen, Redleaf Press acquisitions and development editor, for guidance and assistance for this work. Thanks to each of these reviewers for their significant contributions to this work.

Dennis Angle, BA
Stepparent/Foster Parent
Bowling Green, Kentucky

Karen Burger Cairone, EdM
Trainer/Special Projects/Writer
Devereux Center for Resilient Children
Senior Training and Technical Assistance
   Associate
Education Development Center
Villanova, Pennsylvania

Jill Orthman Hatch, MS
Early Childhood Consultant
Jeremiah, Kentucky

Luis Hernandez, MA
Early Childhood Education Specialist
Miami, Florida

Amy Hood Hooten, EdD
Infant Toddler Specialist
Western Kentucky University
Bowling Green, Kentucky

Linda K. Likins, MA
Executive Director (retired)
Devereux Center for Resilient Children
Villanova, Pennsylvania

Barbara A. Nilsen, EdD
Author, *Week by Week: Documenting the
   Development of Young Children*
Port Crane, New York

Janie Sailors, RN
Health Specialist
Orlando, Florida

Melissa Werner, PhD
Assistant Professor of Early Childhood
   Education
Athens State University
Athens, Alabama

J'Lane Zamora, BS
Owner and Pre-K Teacher
Rocking Horse Daycare and Pre-K
Carrizozo, New Mexico

INTRODUCTION

Addressing children's challenging behaviors can be one of the most emotional and difficult activities you face as an adult working in an early childhood setting. You bring your own beliefs and experiences to every situation, which can make it hard to be objective. Inappropriate or emotional reactions to children's challenging behaviors can turn potential learning situations for children into unnecessary crises. Focusing on helping children learn the skills they need to be successful, instead of focusing on your own feelings, is easier said than done. But it's important to strive toward this goal. Children imitate behavior they see, so you must be able to model self-control and show children how you want them to act in times of conflict or frustration.

This Redleaf Quick Guide suggests strategies you can use for handling some of the most common behavioral issues of young children. It does not, however, provide comprehensive recipes for responding to all situations. Children's behavior is complex. It results from many causes, such as health, physical environment, temperament, experiences, skills, risk factors, and development. Therefore, all adults working with young children should participate with an open mind in ongoing professional development about positive guidance for children. Administrators, teachers, drivers, monitors, substitutes, and volunteers can all benefit from learning more about helping children develop social skills and self-regulation.

Many Challenging Behaviors Represent Typical Development

Your expectations for young children's behavior should be reasonable for their ages and developmental levels. Often the behaviors adults find challenging are typical for certain ages and developmental stages. Young children are learning vocabulary and how language works, so they do not always have the words to express themselves to adults or to one another in socially acceptable ways. Adults like to think of childhood as a magical, carefree time. But it can be frustrating for both children and adults, because children have not yet learned many problem-solving, coping, or self-control skills.

Children's emotions can be intense. Children may not be able to control their actions associated with strong feelings, so they need outlets for their feelings and support in learning self-control. Although children may be curious about others and want to have friends, they may not know how to befriend one another. Their social skills are still evolving. Young children are focused on themselves. They see things from their singular points of view. They also have a naturally increasing need to be independent, which can disturb the routines of a group of children. As typically developing children carve out their identities, they may exhibit every challenging behavior described in this book. During traumatic times, children may temporarily regress and display challenging behaviors that they have previously overcome. The frequency and intensity of children's challenging behaviors can alert you to the possibility that the behaviors are outside the typical developmental framework, and that additional support may be necessary.

Developmental screenings may help determine whether children have potential developmental delays or other issues that impact behavior. Some programs offer developmental screenings with informed consent from families, and other programs make referrals. Screenings alert you only to possible concerns. If screening results indicate a need, more in-depth assessment should follow. Even so, information from screenings may help guide initial action plans to support children in reaching their potential in all areas of development. If challenging behaviors persist and increase during the preschool years, and consistent prevention techniques are unsuccessful, an assessment may need to be considered. Working together, families and teachers can provide positive guidance and support to help young children through challenging times.

Behavior Is Integrated

This Redleaf Quick Guide is intended to be used as needed, not sequentially. It is organized into twelve topics representing common challenging behaviors to help you quickly identify a behavior and useful strategies. But remember, each behavior is related to others. For example, aggression can also be demonstrated through biting, defiance, language, and tantrums. A behavior may begin one way and escalate to include many challenging behaviors. Children may present a challenging behavior in one area or many. Children may also demonstrate a challenging behavior rarely or regularly. If one section of this book is not helpful, consult related areas.

Staying Calm through the Storm

As you use this book to work with children during challenging times, remember to stay calm. Maintaining your composure is your best strategy for dealing with challenging behaviors. Don't get upset, raise your voice, shame children, or make threats. These techniques do not work and will make everyone involved feel more out of control. If you are relaxed, you will be better able to look at the situation objectively, problem solve, and model appropriate behavior. Identifying and using stress-management techniques for yourself is an important behavior-management strategy.

CHAPTER 1: AGGRESSION

OBSERVED BEHAVIOR

- A child is harming others through kicking, hitting, throwing things, pulling hair, or other aggressive actions.

- A child is intimidating others through posturing or physical force.

- A child is destroying property through kicking, throwing, stomping, beating, or other aggressive actions.

APPROPRIATE RESPONSE

The immediate goal is to keep the child from harming herself or others and to help her regain self-control so she can reengage in appropriate activities. The secondary goal is to prevent the child from destroying property.

Harming Others

Infants and Toddlers

- When an infant hits or throws, it is not considered aggressive behavior. Use soothing techniques for the infant and redirect her by introducing a different activity or toy.

- When a toddler behaves aggressively, place yourself between her and others. At eye level, say her name and tell her in a calm but firm voice to stop the aggressive behavior (hitting, pushing, or the like) because it hurts others.

- Examine the victim for physical injury. If the victim has an injury, follow your program procedures.

- Help children regain composure through deep breaths, squeezing balls, back rubs, or other techniques.

- Redirect all toddlers to soothing activities.

Preschoolers

- When a preschooler is aggressive toward another child, place yourself between the children. At eye level, say the name of the child behaving aggressively and tell her in a calm but firm voice to stop the activity (kicking, holding, and so on).

- Suggest that all children involved take some deep breaths to relax.

- Tell the victim that you are there to help. Ask if she is hurt. Examine her for physical injury. If she has an injury, follow your program procedures.

- After you address any injury, help the victim use words to express her own message to the child who was aggressive.

- With the children, discuss possible alternative actions they could have used during the altercation.

- Help each child regain self-control and engage in an activity.

Destructive Behavior

Toddlers

- When a toddler is destructive, slowly approach her. Say her name at eye level and tell her in a calm but firm voice to stop the activity and return the object to its owner, place it on the floor, or give it to you. If necessary, offer to trade for a different object. Thank the child when she cooperates. Help the children relax through deep breaths, squeezing balls, back rubs, or other techniques.

- If another child's work or property was damaged, give her attention and show her sympathy. If possible, help all children involved mend or re-create the work.

- Redirect each child to a soothing activity.

Preschoolers

- When a preschooler is destructive, slowly approach her. At eye level, say her name and tell her in a calm but firm voice to stop the activity and return the object to you or to its owner. If necessary, give the child the option of handing the object to the other child, placing it on the floor, giving it to you, or letting you remove it. Thank her when she cooperates.

- Help the children relax by suggesting deep breathing or other techniques.

- If another child's work or property was damaged, give her attention and show her sympathy.

- Help the child whose work was harmed use words to express her own message to the child who was aggressive.

- When possible, help all children involved mend or re-create what was harmed.

- Redirect each child to a soothing activity when each has regained control.

> **Don't** become angry or aggressive toward the child or instruct other children to use physical aggression as protection. Avoid using labels, such as *brat* or *bully*. Don't tell the victim's family the name of the child who acted aggressively.

Developmental Check

Infants and Toddlers

- Infants may communicate by throwing objects or striking at people. This is typical behavior and is not aggression.

- Toddlers lack the verbal communication skills to let you know what they need or want. They may resort to aggressive acts to communicate.

- Toddlers have limited social skills. They do not understand the concept of sharing resources and space. For example, when there is only one big red truck, and it is the most desirable toy, conflict that could escalate into aggression is likely.

- Toddlers need to be physically active and mentally engaged. If their physical activity is limited for too long, or if they become bored, aggression may result.

Preschoolers

- Preschoolers may have difficulty with a change in routine. Because they express their emotions strongly, the insecurity caused by a changed routine at home or school could escalate into aggression.

- Preschoolers are egocentric. They see things from their own points of view. The individual ways in which they perceive situations limit problem solving. This can cause frustration, leading to aggression.

- As preschoolers' independence increases, it may seem reasonable to them that they should be able to get or do what they want, when they want, and how they want. When you limit their choices, the lack of control they feel may cause their frustration to escalate into aggression.

- Aggressive acts generally decrease during preschool years.

Physical aggression is typical for toddlers and preschoolers, but the intensity may vary. As children learn language, social, and self-control skills, aggression generally decreases. The best ways to prevent children from becoming physically aggressive are to create a community of learners where everyone feels welcome, to supervise children closely, and to plan the play space and activities to address developmental needs.

Observe:
Look at the times, places, and situations in which children exhibit aggressive behaviors to guide you in creating prevention strategies. During daily supervision, recognize when children exhibit behaviors that indicate a need they cannot express verbally, so you can intervene before the behavior escalates into aggression.

Model:
Model cooperation, helpfulness, kindness, and respect. Use appropriate verbal expressions of frustration and avoid any physical actions that could be seen as aggression.

Enhance:
- Provide duplicates of popular toys and ensure adequate play space.

- Introduce activities that help children learn about friendly and gentle touching with permission, such as shaking hands, patting, and hugging.

- Include adequate time and space each day for physical activity, such as running, jumping, dancing, and climbing.

- Provide ample opportunity for language development, including vocabulary to express feelings, desires, and needs.

- Create a warm and accepting learning community where all children feel appreciated and feel that they belong.

- Offer many opportunities for children to practice self-control of their bodies through games such as Simon Says, Hokey Pokey, Red Light/Green Light, or Freeze Tag.

CHAPTER 2: BITING

OBSERVED BEHAVIOR

- A child is biting other children, adults, or himself.

- A child is biting objects that could cause harm to himself or damage to the object.

APPROPRIATE RESPONSE

The immediate priority is to keep the child from harming others or being harmed.

Infants and Toddlers

- When an Infant bites, tell him calmly and firmly that biting hurts, then redirect him by offering a different toy or by moving him to another play space.

- Comfort the child who was bitten and attend to the injury (if necessary) by following your program's procedures. Redirect the child to a soothing activity.

- When a toddler bites another child, place yourself between them and, at the eye level of the child who bit, say in a calm but firm voice, "No biting. It hurts." Have the child who bit take deep breaths to relax.

- Tell the victim that you are there to help, and ask if he is hurt. Examine him for physical injury. If there is an injury, follow your program's procedures.

- Redirect both children to soothing activities.

Preschoolers

- When a preschooler bites someone, place yourself between the two children. At eye level, say in a calm but firm voice to the child who bit, "Stop biting." Suggest deep breaths to help both the children relax.

- Tell the victim that you are there to help, ask if he is hurt, and examine him for physical injury. If there is an injury, follow your program's procedures.

- After addressing any injury, help the victim use words to express his own message appropriately to the child who bit him.

- Once both children are calm, have a brief conversation about alternatives to biting. Give examples of words that children could use.

- Redirect each child to a soothing activity when he has regained control.

- Remain physically close, and supervise the children to reduce the opportunity for more biting.

> **Don't** bite the child back or instruct other children to bite the child back. Don't tell the family of the victim who bit their child. Never label a child as a *biter*.

Developmental Check

Infants and Toddlers

- Infants may bite to communicate if they become overstimulated, frightened, or tired.

- Older infants and toddlers may bite because they need oral stimulation or because they're teething, which causes gum pain.

- Toddlers have strong emotions but lack the verbal communication skills and self-control to express with words what they want or need. Biting may be a result of frustration.

Preschoolers

- Young preschoolers may still be teething, but older preschoolers typically have all their primary teeth.

- Preschoolers are learning new vocabulary, problem-solving strategies, and friendship skills, but if these approaches are not working for them, preschoolers may resort to biting.

- During stressful times, such as a change in family structure or moving to a new home, preschoolers may temporarily regress and display challenging behaviors, such as biting.

Remember that biting is a common behavior for children under three. Biting has many possible causes. The best solution to biting is to supervise children closely and address gum pain, frustration, and other signs of distress early enough to prevent biting.

Observe:
To assist with prevention plans, identify patterns regarding times of day, location, activity, and people associated with biting. Be aware of children who seem to have gum pain or who exhibit behaviors that indicate needs or wants that they cannot communicate verbally.

Model:
Verbally express your frustration appropriately and model cooperation, helpfulness, kindness, and respect. Avoid using any labels, such as *biter*.

Enhance:
- Address teething issues by helping children keep their gums clean. Offer appropriate items to chew, such as wet washcloths, frozen snacks, or liquid-free teething rings.

- Plan a daily schedule that allows children choices, adequate rest, and comforting activities.

- Provide duplicates of popular toys, and ensure adequate play space to reduce frustration.

- Redirect children to another activity when you observe a potential biting situation.

- Present acceptable options as alternatives to biting. Teach children words to use and techniques for sharing. Instruct them to come to an adult for help, if needed.

- Include soothing activities, such as squeezing a ball, stretching, deep breathing, and water play.

CHAPTER 3: CRYING AND WHINING

OBSERVED BEHAVIOR
- A child is crying or whining with apparent need, pain, distress, or fear.

- A child is crying or whining without apparent pain, distress, or fear but is unable to engage in activities.

APPROPRIATE RESPONSE
The first goal is to identify and address any physical need or injury. Any short- and long-term emotional issues should also be identified and addressed.

Infants and Toddlers

- Go to the infant immediately to identify any physical pain, physical need, or emotional issue.

- Address the infant's physical pain according to your program's procedures.

- Address any physical needs, such as hunger, a wet diaper, or other conditions that might make the infant cry.

- Comfort the infant who may be lonely, fearful, or bored. Change the infant's position. Hold, gently rock, sing, coo, and give plenty of attention to the infant. Do not worry about spoiling babies.

- Go to the toddler immediately to identify any physical pain, physical need, or emotional issue.

- Address the toddler's physical pain according to your program's procedures.

- Address the toddler's physical needs, such as hunger, thirst, toilet needs, clothing needs, or other conditions.

- Acknowledge the emotional distress the toddler may be feeling. Offer comfort and reassurance while modeling language to express feelings.

- After she is calm, redirect the toddler to a fun activity.

Preschoolers

- Go to the child immediately to identify any physical pain, need, or emotional issues.

- Address any physical pain according to your program's procedures.

- Acknowledge any emotional distress the child may be feeling and invite her to talk about it. Comfort and reassure the child.

- If the child is crying or whining without apparent physical or emotional reasons, redirect her to an activity she enjoys.

- If the child is crying or whining without apparent physical or emotional reasons, cannot be redirected, and is disturbing other children, locate a place for her to continue crying under supervision of a comforting adult, away from the children she is disturbing.

> **Don't** tell the child to stop crying or whining, that they have no reason to cry or whine, or that only babies cry and whine. Avoid using labels, such as *crybaby*. Never shake a baby or strike a child.

Developmental Check

Infants and Toddlers

- Healthy infants cry! Some cry more than others. They cry to communicate all their needs.

- Infants may cry on and off for a few hours each day during the first weeks of life.

- Crying excessively (more than three hours per day) may indicate a health issue.

- Older infants and toddlers may begin experiencing separation anxiety at about six months. The intensity, longevity, and regularity of separation anxiety are unique to each child.

- Toddlers can use a few words and phrases to communicate, but they lack the vocabulary to express their distress in words.

- Toddlers have and show intense feelings.

Preschoolers

- Younger preschoolers may experience separation anxiety.

- Preschoolers rely on crying less than infants and toddlers do, but still resort to crying and whining in times of distress.

- Children who are trying to speak and understand languages other than their home language may have more difficulty expressing themselves.

- Preschoolers continue to develop and use language in more complex ways, yet may lack the social skills to always use language appropriately.

- Preschoolers are curious and imaginative, which can sometimes lead to fears that adults may consider unreasonable. These fears, however, are real to preschoolers.

Children may sense an adult's tension, which can cause their crying or whining to escalate. Get help or take a break if you cannot stay composed. The best solution to crying and whining is to identify the causes and address them calmly. Try to make children feel welcome and engaged.

Observe:
Look for the behaviors children demonstrate just before crying so you can use prevention techniques, such as reassurance or redirection. Listen to the intensity of the crying to help determine the need being expressed.

Model:
Use language to express feelings. Practice techniques for building friendships and cooperation. Avoid using labels such as *crybaby*.

Enhance:
- Become familiar with your program's procedures for dealing with children's physical pain or injuries. If your program does not have any procedures, be an advocate to address this need.

- Plan a daily schedule that addresses basic needs through timely and responsive feeding, meals, and snacks; adequate drinking water; frequent diaper changing and toilet times; rest opportunities balanced with stimulating activities; fresh air; and adult care and attention.

- Establish arrival rituals that respect children and families saying good-bye, followed by a positive transition into activities that immediately capture the attention of the children. Consider activities and materials that will engage each child—especially those who are experiencing separation anxiety.

- Build a positive relationship with each child. Create an environment where children feel like they belong by saying their names, labeling their personal spaces, allowing them to bring objects from home, and displaying pictures of their families.

- Ensure that you have adequate, consistent, and qualified staffing to address the immediate needs of children.

- Introduce stories and activities that are related to stressful issues the children may be facing, such as the arrival of new siblings, divorce, weddings, or illnesses.

CHAPTER 4: DEFIANCE

OBSERVED BEHAVIOR

- A child says no when asked or instructed by an adult to do or stop doing something.

- A child refuses to cooperate or ignores instructions from an adult to do or stop doing something.

APPROPRIATE RESPONSE

The immediate priority is to keep the child from being harmed or harming others. If harm is not an issue, the behavior (while frustrating to you) may not be critical.

Infants and Toddlers

- Although you may feel that an infant is being defiant, you are feeling only his natural intensity. Meet the infant's needs and develop stress-relief skills for yourself.

- Go to the toddler and, at his eye level, say his name and tell him in an enticing voice what you would like him to do next. Be sure to make it sound fun.

- If the toddler says no, ignore the comment, because it does not necessarily mean he isn't going to follow your direction.

- Show the toddler an object related to the next activity or offer your hand to guide him to the activity area.

- Provide support with statements like "Do you want me to help you?" or "Let's go together."

- If the toddler still resists, acknowledge his feelings and tell him that you understand that he may not want to move to the next activity. Briefly explain why it is important.

Preschoolers

- Go to the preschooler and, at his eye level, say his name. Using a pleasant tone and positive language, tell him what you would like him to do next. For example, instead of saying "Stop playing with that truck," say "Jayden, it's time to put the truck back on the shelf and go outside. Remember, we have trucks in the sandbox."

- Offer choices when possible. For example, offer the child the opportunity to do the task independently or with others, before or after getting his coat on, or "slow like a turtle or fast like a bunny."

- If the child seems unhappy with your direction, acknowledge his feelings. Say something like "I know you really like to play with that truck, but it is time to go outside. What do you think you would like to do outside today?"

- If the child continues to be uncooperative, and safety is not an issue, let him know that you will check back in a minute to see if he is ready then. Try again shortly.

> **Don't** engage in a power struggle by raising your voice, threatening, or arguing with the child. Don't try to physically force the child to do what you want unless safety is an immediate issue. Don't refer to the child as *difficult* or as *a troublemaker*.

Developmental Check

Infants and Toddlers

- Infants react intensely to their immediate needs, including the need to be nurtured and comforted. Defiance is not the issue.

- Healthy toddlers display defiance as they learn about independence. A toddler's personality and skill may influence his level of defiance.

- Toddlers are becoming more independent and expressive about their needs and desires.

- Toddlers say no frequently, even when they do not mean it.

- Toddlers lack the verbal communication skills to let you know politely that they do not want to do something.

- Toddlers are impulsive and lack self-control.

- Toddlers are rooted in the present moment. Change can be difficult.

Preschoolers

- Preschoolers are becoming more capable, Independent, and expressive about their needs and desires.

- Preschoolers are learning new vocabulary and problem-solving strategies for pleading their cases.

- Preschoolers may still be impulsive but are learning self-control.

- Preschoolers are egocentric: they see only their way of looking at things.

- Preschoolers sometimes become deeply engaged in an activity, and it can take a while for them to let it go.

Recognize that defiance is how young children learn about independence. Building positive relationships with children may go a long way toward positive interaction. Carefully evaluate situations and decide whether your instructions are necessary. The best solution to defiant behavior is to avoid power struggles with children.

Observe:
To help prevent defiance, look for patterns in a child's energy level, involvement in activity, and adult interaction associated with defiant behavior. Notice which children are thoroughly engaged in an activity and may have difficulty transitioning.

Model:
Show appropriate ways of verbally expressing frustration. Model teamwork, cooperation, helpfulness, kindness, and respect. Avoid using labels, such as *defiant*, *difficult*, or *troublemaker*.

Enhance:
- Provide a daily schedule in picture form so children can see what comes next. Prepare all children for upcoming changes and deliver a personal reminder to any child who has difficulty with transitions.

- Plan a daily schedule that is flexible enough to accommodate each child's individual rhythm, pace, and choices.

- Include activities that teach respect, kindness, cooperation, helpfulness, and teamwork. Add activities that support self-soothing and build self-control.

- As children are able, involve them in establishing class rules. Once rules are established, discuss why the rules are important for individuals and for the group. Give age-appropriate examples. Expect this discussion to recur.

- Make suggestions and requests of children instead of demands, when possible.

- Give children acceptable choices instead of just commands.

CHAPTER 5: DISENGAGEMENT

OBSERVED BEHAVIOR

- A child rarely engages in meaningful play alone or with other children.

- A child becomes discouraged and gives up easily when a task becomes challenging.

- A child is easily distracted.

APPROPRIATE RESPONSE

The goal is to help children feel successful by becoming involved with and finishing a simple task appropriate to their age and stage of development.

Infants and Toddlers

- Play with the infant by introducing new, age-appropriate toys and games to help her enjoy being involved and playful and to extend her engagement time.

- Use words like *done* and *finished* to introduce infants and toddlers to the concept of completing a task. Say things like "That's the end of the book," "You finished your apple," or "Are you done with the blocks?"

- Offer the toddler cause-and-effect toys that respond—for example, with lights, sounds, or movement—when she plays with them.

- Provide suggestions, encouragement, and help so toddlers learn to finish small tasks in a step-by-step manner.

- Provide toddlers with opportunities for exploration play, such as with dumping blocks.

Preschoolers

- Go to the preschooler who is not engaged and offer two choices that are both acceptable and interesting to her. Say something like "Tonya, would you like to build with blocks or play the colors game?" Go with the child to help her get started and ease away with an encouraging word.

- Go to the preschooler who has abandoned an activity prematurely and give an unobtrusive suggestion such as, "Maybe the piece will fit over here. How about you try that?"

- Go to the preschooler who continues to leave a task unfinished and help her identify small steps that will allow her to finish.

- Go to the preschooler who seems discouraged. Sincerely acknowledge her feelings and then ask some problem-solving questions like "I wonder what would happen if you tried putting the smaller block on top?"

> **Don't** use rewards, such as stickers, when a child engages in or finishes a task. Don't give vague directions like "finish up" or unclear praise like "great job." Don't do the task for the child if she is capable of succeeding with encouragement. Avoid using labels, such as *quitter*.

Developmental Check

Infants and Toddlers

- Infants are generally curious about their own bodies and surroundings.

- Infants learn to engage and become playful when they get appropriate visual and auditory stimulation. They may not engage when stimulation is lacking.

- Toddlers have short attention spans and are not likely to stay with any activity for a long period.

- Toddlers have a growing need to be independent and may not be able to judge their own abilities in advance, resulting in possible frustration.

Preschoolers

- Preschoolers have longer attention spans than toddlers have but do not typically remain engaged for long periods of time.

- Healthy preschoolers are curious about their surroundings. They may become excited and therefore easily distracted.

- Preschoolers are becoming more independent and expressive about what they want to do or do not want to do. If choices don't interest them, they may not engage.

- Preschoolers are learning problem-solving skills but have not mastered them. Frustration may still occur when a preschooler can't successfully solve a problem.

Consider that children have different interests and confidence levels, which may affect engagement. The best solution to a lack of engagement is to make sure you have activities that interest each child. Build a child's confidence and skills by working step by step to accomplish one small activity at a time.

Observe:

Observe to see the time of day and type of activity during which children have trouble engaging or their frustration seems to build, so you can intervene and support their involvement and success. Watch to see the types of activities or materials that each child seems most interested in. Plan accordingly.

Model:

Model engaging in activities and having fun, and celebrate openly when you succeed. Avoid using labels, such as *quitter*.

Enhance:

- Plan some activities that have an ending and are self-correcting, such as puzzles and lotto games, to help children understand the concept of finishing.

- Provide open-ended toys that children can play with for an extended period, such as blocks, creative art supplies, and dramatic play props. Encourage them to explore and try new things.

- Include stories about children trying new things, working until a job is done, and feeling proud in the daily curriculum.

- Add different materials to the classroom on a regular basis to create interest and excitement. Rotate existing materials, add new toys, and include recycled materials. For example, empty paper towel rolls can be used for making music, painting and taping together, building with blocks, and much more.

- Activate prior knowledge by asking children questions about past experiences playing with toys and using equipment at home, in the classroom, or on the playground.

- Encourage teamwork for some activities and support cooperation in completing tasks.

CHAPTER 6: ESCAPING

OBSERVED BEHAVIOR

- A child leaves, unattended by an authorized adult.

- A child hides from adult view or plays out of sight when the group leaves an area.

APPROPRIATE RESPONSE

The immediate priority is to bring the child back into the safety of your supervision and to attend to any injury or emotional crisis, while at the same time maintaining the safety of the other children.

Leaving the Premises

Infants and Toddlers

- Nonmobile infants cannot leave without assistance. Ask authorized adults to sign infants in and out of the program to add a measure of safety and security.

- Ask to see identification and check pickup permission records when any unknown adult attempts to remove an infant or toddler.

- If a toddler leaves the designated play area, move toward him rapidly, calling his name and asking him to stop and wait for you. It is critical that you not sound angry, which may urge him to move away from you and into danger.

- When you are close enough, bend down, open your arms, and ask the toddler to come to you, or reach out your hand to him in order to keep him in your care. Ask if he can tell you or show you where he was going.

- Address the need if it is identified, such as having to go to the bathroom, and let the toddler know he should always stay with an adult.

Preschoolers

- Ask authorized adults to sign preschoolers in and out of the program. Look at identification and check pickup permission records when any unknown adult attempts to remove a preschooler.

- If a preschooler leaves the designated play area, move toward him rapidly, calling him by name and asking him to stop and wait for you. It is critical that you not sound angry, which may urge him to move away from you and into danger.

- If he does not respond or return to you, say that you want to show him a toy, play ball with him, or whatever you think will stop and redirect him.

- Once the child is near you, hold his hand, touch his shoulder, or use some other method of contact so you can gently but physically ensure he will stay safely in your care.

- Address the child's need (for instance, wanting a coat or having to go to the bathroom) if identified. Tell the child that he should stay with an adult and not open the door or gate unless an adult says it is okay. Follow through if you told the child you had a toy to show him or a game to play.

Missing

Toddlers and Preschoolers

- If a child is missing from the group, check the sign-in and sign-out records.

- If the child has not been signed out, ensure that all other children are supervised and then quickly return to the site where the missing child was last seen. While calling his name in a friendly tone, look closely in, behind, and under all furniture, equipment, buildings, and landscaping. Check the child's favorite places, such as the gym or the playground.

- Check with other teachers and staff to see if the child is with another group or is receiving special services, such as speech therapy.

- If the child is not found quickly, contact the program authorities and follow the program's procedures for contacting parent or guardians, and the police for assistance.

- After the child is found, address any physical injuries or emotional issues. Remember that the child may not have intentionally separated from the group and may be frightened. Inform others working with you that the child has been found.

> **Don't** panic, chase a running child, scream, or leave a group of children unsupervised. Avoid using labels, such as *escape artist* or *runner*.

Developmental Check

Toddlers

- Toddlers are learning independence. They typically think they can do much more on their own than they actually can do, so going someplace alone whenever they want to makes perfect sense to them.

- Toddlers may lack the verbal communication skills to tell you what they want. Using their feet to walk somewhere can be a way of communicating their desires or needs.

- Toddlers have only recently learned to run and may feel great delight and power in practicing this new skill.

- Toddlers are playful and may see hiding from adults as lots of fun—their idea of an innocent game of hide-and-go-seek.

- Toddlers imitate adults. If adults are going in and out of the room or area without telling others, toddlers may see nothing wrong with doing the same.

Preschoolers

- Preschoolers have short but growing attention spans and are naturally curious. If play opportunities are not interesting to them, they may seek stimulation elsewhere.

- Preschoolers may flee or hide from things they perceive as scary, such as an insect, a loud noise, or another child.

- Preschoolers may leave the area because they are angry and do not want to participate in an activity.

- Preschoolers are taller, stronger, and have greater fine-motor skills than toddlers have, allowing preschoolers to more easily manipulate doors and gates.

- Preschoolers may be shy or just need time away from the group, and may retreat to a private space where they do not see or hear when the group leaves one space for another.

- Preschoolers may hide from other children or adults to be playful.

Children may leave the group for a variety of reasons. Understanding their needs may help you prevent their escaping in the future. The best solutions include close supervision by an adequate number of adults and clear physical boundaries. Adding door chimes or secure gate latches can also help.

Observe:
Note the days of the week, times of the day, locations, activities, and adults present when children escape or are missing to better evaluate possible prevention techniques. Observe closely to see if children exhibit behaviors that indicate they may have a need that they are not expressing verbally so you can follow up.

Model:
Prior to leaving the group space, inform the other adults of where you are going and when you will return. When you leave, say something like "good-bye" or "see you soon." Doing so models desirable behavior for children and encourages communication and collaboration between adults.

Enhance:
- Become familiar with your program's procedures for ensuring adequate supervision to prevent missing children and for addressing the issue whenever a child is not where he should be. If your program does not have these procedures, be an advocate to address this need.

- Position an adult to always have a clear view of the exit routes, so a child cannot slip out unnoticed. Evaluate staffing patterns for safety and make adjustments as needed for proper supervision and oversight of primary entrances.

- Ensure that doors, gates, and other possible exit routes are securely closed and will create a loud but pleasant sound, such as from chimes or bells, when opened. Consider equipment that may need to be updated to help track movement, prevent missing children, and assist with communication, such as alarm systems, coded keypads, key cards, video surveillance, intercoms, or mobile phones.

- Keep sign-in and sign-out records with you at all times to clearly identify which children are in your care and which ones have been picked up by parents, guardians, or other authorized adults.

- Count all the children when you enter a new space, such as the playground; count heads again prior to leaving; and count the children once more when you arrive at your next destination.

- Involve children in age-appropriate ways to help determine if all classmates are with the group. You can encourage children to look around and see if they can find all their friends, involve them in counting with you during transitions, and review related rules with them.

- Provide information to families regarding safety procedures for drop-off and pickup, including the purpose for the procedures. Post reminder signs about procedures in strategic locations. Seek family support in following procedures and in encouraging their children to follow safety rules.

CHAPTER 7: HYPERACTIVITY

OBSERVED BEHAVIOR

- A child is moving frequently from place to place or running indoors.

- A child is moving body parts constantly, such as shaking a leg or fidgeting hands, even when sitting or standing in one place.

- A child is frequently looking around, appearing to lack focus.

APPROPRIATE RESPONSE

The immediate goal is to help children use their energy appropriately, learn to relax, and engage in meaningful activities to prevent boredom, high levels of frustration, and accidents.

Infants and Toddlers

- Introduce toys and games that encourage the infant to move—to reach, kick, or roll.

- Free infants and toddlers from any unpleasant confinement unless safety is an issue, such as while riding in a car seat.

- Provide safe spaces and abundant time for mobile infants and toddlers to move freely.

- If the toddler seems to be gaining undirected physical momentum, provide a structured opportunity for her to be physically active.

- If the toddler is unable to calm down after physical activity, go to the child individually and, at eye level, say her name and calmly invite her to take some deep breaths or do some slow stretches with you. Try moving to slow music and doing other soothing activities.

Preschoolers

- During learning center time or outside time, go to the child individually and, at her eye level, state her name and suggest activities that may be of interest. Once she shows an interest, begin the activity with her. Then gradually remove yourself, leaving her to continue playing without you.

- If the child is losing focus and her energy level is rising during teacher-directed activities, such as story time, draw her back with physically engaging activities, such as role play or chanting, rather than with commands.

- If the child seems to be gaining undirected physical momentum, provide a structured opportunity for her to be physically active. Let her run or jump in place or move through an obstacle course.

- If the child is unable to engage in an activity after structured physical release, go to the child individually and, at her eye level, state her name and calmly invite her to take some deep breaths with you. Try to transition her into a soothing and relaxing activity, such as water play.

- Break activities into smaller steps to help the child increase focus and complete tasks.

> **Don't** try to make the child be still or maintain eye contact with you. Don't label a child as *hyperactive* or *autistic*. These are medical diagnoses that can be determined only through extensive evaluation by medical professionals.

Developmental Check

Infants and Toddlers

- Healthy infants are active, even before they are mobile. Activity levels will vary among infants.

- After infants become crawlers and walkers, their activity levels increase.

- As with infants, activity levels will vary among toddlers. Toddlers have limited control over their speed and direction as they develop their walking and running skills.

- Five minutes is a long time for a toddler to focus on an activity.

Preschoolers

- Healthy preschoolers are physically active and curious. Activity levels will vary among preschoolers.

- Preschoolers continue to develop and use large-motor skills, such as running.

- Preschoolers become excited and may momentarily forget rules, such as "no running indoors."

- Preschoolers learn through discovery and exploration, which requires activity.

- Ten to fifteen minutes is a long time for preschoolers to focus on an activity before growing fidgety.

Physical activity levels vary among children. Focusing attention and making friends are skills that all young children are learning. The best solution for highly active children is to design spaces, schedules, and curriculum activities to provide many safe opportunities to be active. It is also important to teach social skills and to break tasks into steps to support focus.

Observe:
Identify times in the schedule when activity level and focus may be challenging. Recognize when children are becoming antsy and may need to move so you can adjust the schedule. Watch for children lacking focus to see when they may benefit from additional help.

Model:
Demonstrate being physically active. Model paying attention and listening. Be friendly and courteous to other adults and children.

Enhance:
- Reduce clutter in the learning environment to avoid visual overstimulation. Use sound-absorbing materials to avoid auditory overstimulation.

- Minimize teacher-directed large-group structured times and make them optional for children. This will encourage you to make all large-group activities interactive and fun.

- Incorporate large-motor opportunities into the indoor learning environment, including a small station that is always available. For example, set up a circle where children can jump up and down in place or a spot to toss beanbags.

- Encourage focus by using scaffolding techniques, such as giving hints, activating prior knowledge, using visual aids and gestures, and encouraging cooperative work.

- Support social skills and friendship building by having shared physical space and materials. For example, begin by placing infants where they can see one another, provide duplicate toys so toddlers can play with matching toys side by side, and include space for several preschoolers to play at the water table at the same time.

- Build children's confidence by establishing positive relationships, setting realistic goals, helping them succeed, giving genuine compliments, acknowledging their feelings, celebrating success, and setting appropriate limits.

CHAPTER 8: LANGUAGE

OBSERVED BEHAVIOR

- A child is raising his voice to a disturbing level.

- A child is using inappropriate language.

- A child is using words or tones that intimidate or are hurtful to other children.

APPROPRIATE RESPONSE

The immediate priority is to calm and redirect the child while minimizing the effect of his shouting or inappropriate language on other children.

Infants and Toddlers

- When an infant makes loud noises or screams, go to him immediately and offer comfort by holding him and talking in soothing tones. Address any physical needs.

- When a toddler is loud, observe him to determine if he seems injured, angry, frustrated, or excited. Immediately address physical injury, following the procedures of your program. For emotional situations, acknowledge the child's feelings, whisper to him to use a softer voice, and ask if he can show you what caused the outburst so you can help him address the issue appropriately.

- When a toddler uses inappropriate language, ignore what he said and redirect his language by saying a substitute word that sounds silly or funny. Continue to redirect him to a fun activity.

- If a toddler uses words about toileting frequently and in inappropriate situations, tell him that "we whisper those words" or that "we use those words only in the bathroom."

- If a toddler uses hurtful words or tones to intimidate children, ask him to please stop, because hurtful words or tones hurt feelings. Help all children involved gain composure. According to their language ability, encourage the victims to express their feelings and encourage the child who used hurtful words or tones to listen. Show the children alternative methods they could have used to resolve their issue and then engage them in other activities.

Preschoolers

- When a preschooler is loud, observe him to determine if he seems injured, angry, frustrated, or excited. Immediately address physical injury, following the procedures of your program. Ask the child who is loud but not injured to please speak (or make whatever sound he's making) more softly. Acknowledge his feelings by saying something like "Casey, you seem upset. Tell me about it." Engage in a conversation and help him resolve the issue.

- If the preschooler frequently raises his voice to a disturbing level after you have addressed his doing so several times, ensure that safety is not an issue and redirect him to a new activity. Encourage other children to continue their activities.

- When a preschooler uses inappropriate language, ignore it, and redirect the child to another activity. If other children call your attention to it, tell them that you heard it, but say no more. If the inappropriate language becomes frequent, go to the child and calmly and quietly say something like "Please do not use that word." Give the child an alternative word to use.

- When a preschooler uses words or tones that intimidate or show lack of respect for other children, place your body between the children involved in the conflict. Assure the child or children who were verbally assaulted that you are there for them. Tell the child who is being offensive to please stop, because his language is hurtful. Help the children relax by encouraging them to take deep breaths or hum a song. Facilitate a conversation between the children about their feelings and alternative problem-solving methods, then redirect them to activities.

> **Don't** shout back at the child or instruct other children to shout back. Don't emphasize the behavior or shame the child for using words you do not consider appropriate. Avoid using labels, such as *potty mouth*, *loudmouth*, or *bully*.

Developmental Check

Infants and Toddlers

- Infants communicate through their cries, which can become loud.

- Toddlers are continuing to learn about language and may be experimenting with voice level, tones, words, and sounds, such as squeals.

- Toddlers may be learning new words about their genitals and bathroom functions through their toilet training, and they have not yet learned discretion.

- Toddlers lack the language to negotiate well and may intimidate other children to get their own way.

Preschoolers

- Children learn language through imitation. Sometimes preschoolers use language they have heard without understanding its meaning.

- Preschoolers play with words, including words that may displease adults. They test the sounds and power of words.

- Preschoolers may become excited, fearful, angry, or frustrated and use loud or inappropriate language to express their feelings. A child may lack the skills to express his feelings appropriately.

- Preschoolers may have experienced success at getting positive or negative attention from adults by using inappropriate language or screaming. If they feel it works for them, they may continue.

- Preschoolers may lack the language or social skills to negotiate well and may intimidate other children to get their own way.

A noisy group of children may indicate active engagement and should not be discouraged. However, children who are excessively loud or intimidating should be taught appropriate communication and social skills. The best solution for children using loud or inappropriate language is to help them develop respect for one another, appropriate ways of expression, and coping strategies.

Observe:
Determine any patterns that exist concerning inappropriate language or tones. Notice when children seem to be frustrated, angry, or in the initial stages of conflict with others, so you can help them before outbursts occur. Look closely to identify children who are intimidated but do not tell you.

Model:
Use pleasant and appropriate ways of communicating verbally with other adults, individual children, and the group. Avoid calling loudly across the room or playground or speaking in unkind tones. Model peaceful problem-solving and negotiation skills.

Enhance:

- Provide time in the schedule and room in the environment for children to be loud—whether that means joyful squealing, roaring laughter, giggling, groaning, or other sounds.

- Incorporate relevant materials, such as books about bullying, name-calling, cooperation, and friendship. Children may imitate what they see or hear, making it important to select more positive examples than lessons based on negative examples.

- As a substitute for inappropriate language exploration, provide children with a rich vocabulary that includes multisyllabic words, silly sounds, rhymes, and words from various languages.

- Include activities for a small group of children that encourage cooperation, such as a simple board game that requires taking turns. Model cooperation and comment on specific ways that children are being cooperative, such as passing cards or game pieces, waiting their turn, or complimenting each other.

- Sings songs or chant rhymes at soft, medium, and then loud volumes to help children compare sound levels and learn to control their voices.

- Show a small group of children a simple puppet show demonstrating friendship skills, such as greeting each other kindly, inviting someone to play, or working together to move a block to another location. Let children take turns repeating the puppet show or role-playing the story.

CHAPTER 9: SEPARATION ANXIETY

OBSERVED BEHAVIOR
- A child cries and whines when a parent or guardian leaves her in your care.
- A child reverts to behaviors of younger children and refuses to participate or interact.

APPROPRIATE RESPONSE
The immediate priority is to acknowledge the feelings the child is expressing, provide comfort, and transition her to an enjoyable activity.

Infants and Toddlers

- Hold the infant and provide physical comfort while talking or singing soothingly. Show the infant something visually stimulating, such as bubbles, a mobile, or a toy.
- Reach your arms out and offer to hold the toddler. If she does not want to be held, sit next to her.
- Acknowledge her feelings and say something like "You look unhappy that your auntie left."
- Encourage her to look at a photograph of her loved one posted in the room or in a class picture album.
- Reassure her that her loved one will come back and that while she waits, she can play. Offer a toy that the toddler has shown interest in previously or that a family member or guardian has informed you she likes.

Preschoolers

- Go to the preschooler who is distressed and sit near her. Acknowledge her feelings and invite her to talk about them. Say something like "You seem pretty upset that your dad had to go to work today. Can you tell me about it?" Let the child know her feelings are okay.
- Ask if a hug or back rub might help her feel better. Provide that physical comfort if requested.

- Reassure the child that her family member or guardian will come back. If you know when, show her on the clock or on a daily picture schedule.

- Remind her about the photographs of her loved one on the wall, in a class album, or in her cubby that she can look at anytime.

- Suggest an activity that the child has shown an interest in previously or that the family member or guardian has informed you she likes. Begin the activity with the child to re-direct her.

> **Don't** encourage the family member or guardian to sneak off. Don't take the child's distress personally or as a sign that you are not a good teacher. Don't tell the child that big girls and boys do not cry. Don't tell her to stop crying. Don't try to hold the child if she resists physical contact.

Developmental Check

Infants and Toddlers

- Separation anxiety is not an issue for young infants, but it may begin to occur around six months.

- The level of separation anxiety for infants and toddlers will vary. It may be influenced by many things, including the child's temperament.

- Older infants and toddlers can be redirected to activities within a few minutes of their loved ones' departure.

- While toddlers are increasingly interested in independence, they may have times of separation anxiety. They also lack the vocabulary to express their feelings about separation anxiety.

Preschoolers

- Some younger preschoolers may suffer from separation and stranger anxiety, but most have adjusted to temporary separations.

- Older preschoolers who have not experienced separation anxiety for months may feel it renewed when changes occur in their lives, such as family illness, divorce, or a new baby in the family.

- Preschoolers are curious and imaginative, which can sometimes lead to fears that adults consider unreasonable. To the child, however, these fears are real. New fears may cause separation anxiety to recur.

- Preschoolers continue to develop and use language in more complex ways and are developing a better understanding of time, so a discussion about separation anxiety is possible.

Crying, clinging, and even tantrums are typical for children during separation anxiety, but the intensity may vary from child to child. The best solution for separation anxiety is to be prepared for the children's arrivals and warmly welcome each child by name as she arrives. Address any anxiety in a sensitive way for the child and adult.

Observe:
Recognize when individual children experience more separation anxiety so you can be better prepared to assist. Try to determine if the behavior follows patterns. Is it more likely on certain days of the week, or when the child arrives later or earlier in the day?

Model:
Offer positive greetings, say good-bye cheerfully, use language to express feelings, and become engaged in activities with children.

Enhance:
- Encourage family members and guardians to allow enough time for a smooth, unrushed drop-off.

- Provide continuity of care by having consistent teachers. Limit the number of adults to avoid overwhelming children.

- Allow children to bring items from home that may help soothe and comfort them.

- Include family photographs posted on the walls, in classroom photo albums, or in electronic picture frames that rotate images.

- Play hide-and-go-seek with objects. Point out how each object is still there even when the child can't see it. Play hide-and-go-seek with children who are old enough to understand the game.

- Help families create a happy ritual for drop-off and pickup that their children can anticipate and practice. Rituals may be a saying, such as "Love you oodles and boodles," or blowing kisses as the adult leaves.

CHAPTER 10: SEXUALIZED BEHAVIOR

OBSERVED BEHAVIOR

- A child excessively self-stimulates his genitals.

- A child compares his genitals to those of other children or displays his genitals publicly.

- A child engages in sexual role play.

APPROPRIATE RESPONSE

The immediate priority is to prevent children from touching one another's genitals and to avoid overreaction to typically developing self-exploration or self-stimulation.

Infants and Toddlers

- When an infant is exploring or self-stimulating his genitals, ensure that the child does not harm himself, but otherwise allow it. If older children ask about it, explain that the baby is learning about his body.

- When a toddler engages in self-stimulation, check to see if he needs to use the bathroom or is hurting in any way, so you can make a medical referral if needed. If no bathroom need or medical concern exists, then ignore self-stimulation. If it is excessive, redirect the child to an activity that requires his hands.

- When a toddler compares his genitals to another child's, go to the children quickly to prevent them from touching each other and say something like "Max, you noticed that Jan has a vagina and you have a penis. Please do not touch each other's private body parts." Then help them become interested in an activity that may capture their attention.

- If a toddler has his pants down and is displaying his genitals, calmly investigate to see why. Help him with any physical needs, such as soothing itching insect bites or changing wet clothes. If you can't identify any health needs, say something like "Bryson, please pull your pants up. Your penis is a private body part."

Preschoolers

- When a preschooler engages in self-stimulation, ignore it unless the behavior becomes excessive, drawing the attention of others or interfering with the child's routine. If excessive self-stimulation occurs, redirect the child to another activity that requires the use of his hands. In private, ask the child if his penis (or her vagina) hurts so you can determine if a referral is needed.

- When a preschooler compares his genitals to another child's, and it appears there may have been physical contact, go to the children and say something like "Rashid, you noticed that Sarah has a vagina and you have a penis. Boys and girls have some different body parts that are private. Please do not touch each other's private body parts." Answer any questions briefly but honestly, and then help them become interested in an activity that may capture their attention.

- If a preschooler has his pants down and is displaying his genitals, calmly investigate to see why. Assist with any physical needs, such as pulling his pants up and moving into the bathroom, soothing itching insect bites, or changing wet clothes. If no health needs are identified, say something like "Bryson, please pull your pants up. Your penis is a private body part."

> **Don't** insist that the child stop sexual self-exploration or self-stimulation unless physical harm is evident. Don't show shock or shame the child.

Developmental Check

Infants and Toddlers

- Infants are curious and explore their world by exploring their own bodies first. Self-stimulation is typical.

- During toilet training, toddlers are focused on the genital area and its function.

- Toddlers recognize that self-stimulation of the genital area feels good. Like anything else that feels good to them (thumb sucking, rubbing their favorite blanket, or feeling their mother's hair, for example), they seek it out, especially when they need comfort.

- Toddlers lack modesty and have not yet learned about privacy. Their limited language skills may result in their using their hands to explore things they cannot ask about verbally.

Preschoolers

- Preschoolers are still focused on themselves but have a growing interest in others. They are learning about ways that they are similar and different from one another, including gender differences.

- Typically, preschoolers have learned more coping skills than toddlers, but they may still touch their genitals to soothe, comfort, or calm themselves.

- Preschoolers may role-play sexual scenes they have personally experienced, witnessed, or watched on television shows and movies.

Self-exploration is a natural part of development and should not be prevented. Providing a comforting and nurturing environment that addresses the children's emotional needs may minimize the need for self-stimulation. Close observation and supervision should prevent violent or aggressive sexualized behavior.

Observe:
Notice whether children demonstrate sexualized behavior that is not appropriate for their age. Make referrals for medical assistance or counseling as needed. If you suspect sexual abuse, you must report it.

Model:
Model being comfortable with your own body and sexuality by using correct names for body parts, answering questions briefly but honestly, and remaining calm when children self-stimulate or ask questions about sexuality.

Enhance:
- In the daily curriculum, include activities that help teach relaxation and self-soothing techniques, such as deep breathing, stretching, moving to soft music, water play, and singing.

- Incorporate in the daily curriculum opportunities for children to learn about privacy, modesty, and respect for their own and one another's bodies.

- Use correct terminology for genitals and do not avoid or dismiss questions and concerns children have. See these as teaching opportunities to help children learn to accept and respect others.

- Read books about hugs, shaking hands, and other socially appropriate touches. Let children practice asking each other if they can shake hands, hug, or give a high five. Stress that they should follow through only when they receive permission.

- Talk with children, as they are able to understand, about personal space. Help them understand that their cubbies are their own spaces and that it is important not to touch anyone's space but their own. Update names and decorations to make the cubbies personal.

- Introduce the idea of knocking by sharing knock-knock jokes, knocking a pattern for children to repeat, or in other ways. Follow up by talking about when and where people should knock to show respect for privacy.

CHAPTER 11: SHYNESS

OBSERVED BEHAVIOR

- A child plays alone or near other children most of the time, rarely joining others.

- A child rarely engages in meaningful play alone or with other children and demonstrates quiet behaviors of distress, such as rocking or thumb sucking.

APPROPRIATE RESPONSE

The immediate goal is to comfort a child who may feel rejected and help her build confidence and skills in approaching others to play. It is also important to respect the choice of a child when she prefers to play independently and to recognize cultural differences in interactions.

Infants and Toddlers

- Point out other children and adults to infants and model social behaviors. For example, say something like "India, look at Mack. He is playing with his toes. You have toes too. Here they are."

- Limit the number of new people the infant or toddler is exposed to at one time. Provide comfort and support if she seems distressed by strangers.

- Go to the toddler who is interested in toys another child is using and offer a duplicate or alternative toy. Encourage the toddlers to play side by side.

- Go to the toddler who is not welcomed by another toddler or preschooler and acknowledge her feelings of disappointment or anger. Help her negotiate a way to contribute to the existing play group or redirect her to another activity.

- Encourage toddlers to play short cooperative games, such as rolling a ball back and forth, to introduce them to group play.

- Comfort any toddler showing signs of distress and redirect her to an activity of interest.

Preschoolers

- Go to the preschooler who is not welcomed into a group and acknowledge her feelings of disappointment or anger.

- Suggest ways to help the child enter the group. Examples include being helpful, getting toys for the group, playing a role that is not yet claimed, or suggesting ideas.

- If the child is unable to enter the group with your suggestions, offer to play something of interest with the child. Encourage her to invite others to join.

- Go to the preschooler who is playing independently and ask if you can play. Try to assess social skills to determine if she needs assistance or prefers independent play.

- If the child is uninvolved in any activity and is showing signs of distress, try to identify any concerns and reassure her, then attempt to engage the child in an activity that interests her.

> **Don't** overlook quiet children who do not overtly demand your attention. Don't chastise children for not playing with others or pressure them to interact more. Don't require other children to include timid or withdrawn children in their play. Don't label children as *shy*, *timid*, or *withdrawn*.

Developmental Check

Infants and Toddlers

- Infants and toddlers tend to be curious about their surroundings, including the people in their environment.

- Older infants and toddlers may experience separation and stranger anxiety.

- Toddlers do not see the point of view of others and often cannot share or cooperate well.

- Toddlers use a few words and phrases to communicate but lack the vocabulary to express friendship.

- Toddlers have and show intense feelings, which may be an obstacle to friendship.

Preschoolers

- Younger preschoolers may suffer from separation anxiety and stranger anxiety.

- Children who have a different home language from most of the other children may have more difficulty appropriately expressing their interest in friendship.

- Preschoolers continue to develop and use language in more complex ways.

- Preschoolers lack the social skills to always use language appropriately.

- Preschoolers are learning and may be practicing problem-solving and negotiating skills.

Some children are naturally friendlier than others. A wide range of social interaction is healthy. The best solution for supporting timid and withdrawn children is to provide an environment of acceptance and cooperation and to teach friendship skills.

Observe:
Notice when children seem to be shy or withdrawn. Try to determine whether they are happy playing alone or if they seem to want to play with others but cannot successfully enter group play situations.

Model:
Demonstrate how to enter a group of playing children and how to invite others to play. Use positive language when interacting with others.

Enhance:
- Build a positive relationship with each child. Gently encourage children to practice social skills and assertiveness with you so you can encourage them and give feedback.

- Actively teach children how to make friends and play together. Plan activities, such as class murals, that encourage children to build friendships and work cooperatively.

- In the daily curriculum, include stories and activities that are related to friendship, teams, and courage.

- Role-play with children to help them practice social skills, such as inviting someone to play or displaying an act of kindness.

- Provide a wide range of leadership opportunities for all children on a regular basis. However, avoid insisting that children assume leadership in ways that make them uncomfortable.

- Create an inclusive, equitable community of learners. Ensure that everyone is represented through materials and displays and is treated in a fair and kind way.

CHAPTER 12: TANTRUMS

OBSERVED BEHAVIOR
- A child is kicking, swinging his arms, throwing things, or thrashing his whole body on the ground or floor.

- A child is screaming, ranting, crying, or holding his breath during the physical behaviors mentioned above.

APPROPRIATE RESPONSE
The immediate priority is to keep the child from harming himself or others and to support him in regaining self-control.

Infants and Toddlers

- When an infant uses his body and voice to communicate emotions and needs, address his cries promptly and warmly.

- When a toddler demonstrates tantrum behaviors, observe from a few feet away, acting busy unless it appears the child is about to inflict immediate harm on himself, others, or property. Assure other children who may inquire about the tantrum that the child will be okay. Tell the other children to continue with what they are doing or calmly move them to another adequately supervised area.

- In the event of potential harm, get help from another adult to supervise, reassure, and treat any injuries to other children and to relocate these children if needed. Try to remove any object the toddler is using to inflict injury on himself, others, or property.

- After the tantrum has stopped, slowly move physically closer to the child and, when he seems ready to accept it, help him continue to relax through deep breathing, humming, back rubbing, hugging, cuddling soft toys, or other methods.

- Once the child is composed, help him clean up any mess created by the tantrum, and then help him reenter the group successfully.

Preschoolers

- When a preschooler demonstrates tantrum behaviors, observe from a few feet away, acting busy unless it appears the child is about to inflict immediate harm on himself, others, or property. Assure other children who may inquire about the tantrum that the child will be okay. Tell the other children to continue with what they are doing or calmly move them to another adequately supervised area.

- In the event of potential harm, get help from another adult to supervise, reassure, and treat any injuries to other children and to relocate these children if needed. Try to remove any object the child is using to inflict injury on himself, others, or property.

- After the tantrum has stopped, slowly move physically closer to the child and, when he seems ready to accept it, help him continue to relax through deep breathing, humming, back rubbing, hugging, cuddling soft toys, or other methods.

- Avoid talking about the tantrum, but ask the child how he is feeling. Encourage but do not pressure him to talk about his anger, fear, and other emotions. Validate his feelings, but do not talk about the tantrum behavior. Give him ideas for how to solve the problem that caused the tantrum, in case it occurs again.

- Once the child is composed, help him clean up any mess created by the tantrum, and then help him reenter the group successfully.

> **Don't** give attention to the child during the tantrum unless it's necessary for safety reasons. Don't make fun of the child or call him a baby. Don't try to physically restrain the child unless you have received specialized training or written permission appropriate to your state's requirements, and it is necessary for safety reasons.

Developmental Check

Infants and Toddlers

- Infants do not have tantrums. They use their expressions, bodies, and voices to communicate emotions and needs.

- Toddlers are learning independence and begin to show defiant behavior when things do not go their way.

- Toddlers lack the verbal communication skills to let you know what they want or need and may resort to tantrums to communicate.

- Toddlers lack self-control and have not yet learned skills to help them cope with their emotions.

- Toddlers imitate adults and other children and may have tantrums if they have seen out-of-control behaviors.

Preschoolers

- Preschoolers are less likely to have tantrums than toddlers are, since preschoolers typically have greater language skills and have increased self-control. However, younger preschoolers have tantrums at times.

- Preschoolers may have difficulty with a change in routine or daily transitions, and the frustration could escalate into a tantrum.

- Preschoolers are egocentric; they see things from their own points of view. Therefore, problem solving is limited to the way a preschooler perceives a situation. This could cause high levels of frustration, leading to a tantrum.

- As a preschooler's independence increases, it may seem reasonable to the child that he should be able to get or do what he wants, when he wants, and how he wants. When choices are limited, frustration at the lack of control may escalate into a tantrum.

Tantrums are typical for toddlers who have limited language and self-control skills, but tantrums can vary in intensity. The best solution for tantrums is to keep your composure and keep all children safe during the tantrum. Help the child relax and successfully reenter the group after the tantrum, and place ongoing focus on language and self-control skills.

Observe:
Learn more about why different children have tantrums and what their behavior looks like immediately before a tantrum, so you can help the children find alternative ways to express themselves. Notice if children exhibit behaviors that may indicate a need they cannot express verbally and follow up.

Model:
Use appropriate ways of expressing your frustration verbally. Model and explain coping and problem-solving skills.

Enhance:
- When possible, be flexible with transitions between activities, especially for children who take more time or less time than others.

- In the daily curriculum, include activities and materials that help teach communication, coping, and problem-solving skills.

- Incorporate the opportunity to work off frustration through physical activities, such as running, skipping, jumping, dancing, exercises, beating a drum, or pounding clay.

- Include stress-reducing and soothing activities in the daily schedule, such as yoga, stretches, breathing, or softly chanting soothing sounds.

- During positive interactions, ensure time to really listen to, understand, and enjoy each child. Be every child's advocate in the learning community.

- Offer choices to and control over as many things as possible to help children develop decision-making skills and to help children feel empowered. For example, do they want to use crayons or markers?

CHAPTER 13: MOVING BEYOND THE CRISIS

Systematic Observation

As an early childhood professional, you watch children all day long. But you may be so busy organizing daily activities that it's often a challenge to *really see* each child individually. It's even less likely that you'll see the quiet children who exhibit internalizing behaviors, such as withdrawing from situations, hiding, or failing to engage with others. By closely observing and objectively recording what you see and hear, you can learn a great deal about the children in your group and their behaviors. Observing may help you better understand individual children and see their strengths, interests, family traditions, needs, fears, and other factors that contribute to their personalities and behaviors. Systematic observation helps you see how often a specific behavior really occurs. For example, it may seem like a behavior occurs frequently, when in reality it happens only on the playground, just on Tuesdays, when two specific children play together, when you alter the schedule, or the like. There are many ways to record behavior, including the following:

- anecdotal notes

- running notes

- video recordings

- audio recordings

- checklists

- rating scales

- frequency counts

- time samplings

Give systematic observation a try. See what you can learn about the children you work with. As you notice patterns, you may be able to predict when a challenging behavior is likely to occur, and you can take steps to prevent it.

Children Learn from Meaningful and Appropriate Experiences

Young children depend on adults to teach them what they need to be successful and happy. When you work with young children, *everything* you do and say is teaching. You may think that you must focus all of your teaching time on academic activities, such as literacy and math. However, it's critical that you plan for the needs of the whole child and also teach social skills, support emotional development, and encourage physical activities. Often you can integrate academic skills into social, emotional, and physical development. For example, reading a story aloud about an emotional situation integrates literacy with emotional development. Do not lose sight of the value of addressing a child's total development.

Helping children learn appropriate behavior is much like helping them learn any other new skill, and it requires your planning and support. Young children do not yet understand the concept of sharing. Keep this in mind when you design the physical space. Include adequate room for play so children won't be crowded. Try to have duplicates of popular toys. Be sure to include materials that encourage self-expression and communication. Provide a daily schedule that is stimulating but not rushed. It should allow for adequate physical activity. Do not expect young children to sit still for very long. They should be actively involved in fun-filled activities that teach them about getting along in this world. Create a curriculum that is individualized and addresses the strengths, interests, and needs of each child. Help children build their vocabularies so they can use words instead of aggressive behavior. Include conflict-resolution, coping, and problem-solving skills in the curriculum. Teach students about friendly and gentle touching, such as shaking hands, patting, and hugging. Help children learn about respect and kindness.

Building Positive Relationships

Building a positive relationship with each child is important. It may even help reduce challenging behaviors. To build a positive relationship, it's important to recognize the child's individual interests, needs, temperament, and cultural background. Relationships are not built overnight; they take time and effort.

Continuity of care makes such a big difference. For this reason, many administrators schedule staff to work with the same children each day. Some programs even arrange for children to stay with the same teacher for years. Having the same adult be responsible for the care of specific children over a long period of time facilitates close attachment. You are more likely to be supportive and understanding of children with whom you have connected positively. Children, for their part, are more likely to be cooperative during difficult times if they have a bond with you. A positive relationship tends to make the challenging times go more smoothly for both you and the child.

Welcoming families into the program and establishing a positive relationship from the start is an important strategy for supporting all children. Ongoing communication with families helps build good relationships. Keep families informed of positive daily activities and events. Provide families with information about children's typical development. Inform families of program policies and procedures, as well as of any state or national mandates about discipline. When you have a behavioral concern, avoid alarming families. Instead, help them understand whether the challenging behavior is developmentally typical for the child's age. Do not imply that families should punish their children at home for behavior exhibited in your care. If a child's challenging behaviors do not respond to positive guidance techniques and disrupt the learning of the child or others, work with the family to establish a plan that will help the child learn the skills needed for more positive behavior.

Respecting Diversity

Some of the families of the children you work with may look and act differently from your own family. Yours may be richer or poorer, larger or smaller. You may have one father instead of two, or a granny rather than a nana. Maybe you were adopted, raised by your aunt, or in foster care. You may have no siblings or a whole bunch. Your family may feel differently about religion, celebrate other holidays, speak another language, and practice "strange" traditions. All these family characteristics and traditions contributed to who you are now and to what you believe. Although you may not identify with the families of the children you work with, it is important to learn about, understand, and respect them. You want others to respect your family values, and as a professional, you must respect family values that are different from your own.

Identifying When a Referral Is Needed

Escalating and dangerous behavioral and health concerns may need to be referred to other professionals. Follow your program's procedures. To determine if a referral may be appropriate, conduct systematic observation and document objectively. Be careful to consider a child's cultural and linguistic backgrounds and avoid stereotyping or creating bias based on a behavioral incident. You must always strictly respect confidentiality and take care to provide objective information for referrals only after you have received informed family consent. If your program does not have funds to pay for such a resource, the referral may simply be a suggestion to a family to obtain assistance for their child. If free or income-based resources exist in your area, share that contact information with the family.

Working with Other Professionals

Most people agree that two heads are better than one. Other professionals may be able to assist you with providing positive guidance for young children. It can feel lonely and frustrating to go it alone, so seek help and advice for both yourself and the children you care for.

Early Childhood Professionals

A peer, supervisor, representative from your local resource and referral agency, or a local college or university instructor are possible sources of insight. Sometimes having another pair of eyes look at the physical arrangement of the space and provide feedback can help you enhance the learning environment and thus increase positive behavior. Do you have too much open space? Do you have so much furniture that the space is crowded? Are the toys easily accessible, and is it clear where they should be returned? Do you have sound-absorbing materials to control noise?

Another set of eyes reviewing the daily schedule and curriculum activities may help you see ways to adjust the schedule or add more meaningful experiences for children. Routinely including activities that help children learn skills that may reduce challenging behaviors can be helpful. Do the children seem pressured and rushed or comfortable and secure? Are the children engaged in the activities and materials provided, or are they moving around aimlessly and acting bored? Is the sound in the room that of happy exploration or of frustration? Are children using language to express themselves and resolve conflict? Are children using problem-solving skills?

Administrators

Your supervisor, board of directors, or funding source may have resources or the ability to help you network with others to address unmet needs. Communicating with your administration about resources to support positive guidance is essential. Your need may be significant and costly, such as another adult to help ensure the safety of children. But sometimes inexpensive additions can make a world of difference—a secure latch to keep children from opening unsafe spaces; a chime to alert you to someone entering or leaving; a second play truck to reduce conflict and help children engage in meaningful side-by-side play; a storybook to help a child work through feelings about the new baby at home; puppets to encourage a child to express emotions in safe and acceptable ways. Requesting resources to support positive behavior allows administrators to plan for and seek needed funds.

Health Professionals

A family physician, pediatrician, dentist, audiologist, counselor, psychologist, or other health professional may be able to help identify possible reasons for challenging behaviors and assist with solutions.

Health issues can sometimes cause challenging behaviors. For example, children may bite because of gum discomfort. A dentist or pediatrician may be more likely to recognize this issue than a teacher would be. Teachers observing a child consistently scratching her genital area may see it as sexual exploration, but a family physician may see that it could be insect bites, a rash, or another skin condition in need of treatment. An audiologist may be able to diagnose hearing impairment or ear infection in a child who does not respond to directions or who speaks loudly. Counselors may be important resources if challenging behaviors escalate and become dangerous. Health professionals bring specialized perspectives and training, helping expand the assessment of the situation and often leading to a more comprehensive solution.

Being Ready for Emergencies

Emergencies may occur as a result of challenging behaviors even when all possible preventive techniques have been exercised. Knowing the steps to take during emergencies will save valuable time when it counts most. Know your program's policies and procedures so you can react appropriately and quickly. Having a source of communication to summon additional support is critical. Mobile phones, intercoms, walkie-talkies, or other such devices should be available at all times.

Taking Care of Yourself

As you work toward learning how to better handle the behavioral challenges you face, remember that taking care of yourself is also important. One way to take care of yourself is through continued professional development. Reading journals, watching DVDs, exploring early childhood websites, attending workshops, enrolling in college classes, and finding a mentor will help you become more knowledgeable about typical child development and confident in addressing challenging behaviors. Understanding, supporting, and contributing to your program's policies and procedures will help you know what to do in difficult situations. Asking for resources and help when you need them shows maturity. It takes a team to deal with difficult issues. Stay well. If you are tired, sick, or burned out, you will have a harder time dealing with behavioral challenges. Take a vacation, put your feet up, soak in the tub, and refresh yourself personally and professionally.

RESOURCES FOR ONGOING PROFESSIONAL GROWTH

Online Resources

Center on the Social and Emotional Foundations for Early Learning (CSEFEL)

www.csefel.vanderbilt.edu

Initially funded by the Office of Head Start and the Child Care Bureau, CSEFEL has a wealth of free online resources, including videos; training modules; *What Works* Briefs, handouts that provide brief research-based information about preventing challenging behaviors; Book Nooks, guides that provide ideas for using storybooks to support social and emotional development; Scripted Stories for Social Situations, which help children understand social skills; and posters to use as cue cards for teaching social skills. The resources are based upon the Pyramid Model for Supporting Social Emotional Competence in Infants and Young Children. Although the initial funding has ended, CSEFEL resources are also available through the Pyramid Model Consortium at www.pyramidmodel.org.

Devereux Center for Resilient Children

www.centerforresilientchildren.org

Devereux offers free online support materials related to social and emotional development, challenging behaviors, and building resilience. Products are for sale through the Kaplan Early Learning Company and include strengths-based social and emotional assessment kits for birth through school age, challenging behavior programs, and resources for adult resilience. The award-winning book *Flip It: Transforming Challenging Behaviors* is a Devereux product. *Facing the Challenge: Working with Children Who Use Challenging Behaviors,* a two-part DVD developed in cooperation with Video Active Productions and the National Association for the Education of Young Children, is another instructional tool to help educators work better with children who present challenging behaviors. A variety of training options are available.

Early Childhood Learning and Knowledge Center (ECLKC)

https://eclkc.ohs.acf.hhs.gov

This Head Start site offers resources on a wealth of topics, including challenging behaviors and related issues, such as literacy, social, and emotional development. Print and multimedia resources (podcasts, webinars, and videos) are included. In addition to its training and technical assistance (T/TA) resources, this site has sections about grant oversight, policy and regulation, collaboration and partnerships, and data and reports.

National Association for the Education of Young Children (NAEYC)

www.naeyc.org

NAEYC is a professional association that provides free online resources related to many topics, including child guidance and discipline. NAEYC resources are organized into topics, and two topics related to challenging behaviors are positive guidance and suspension and expulsion. NAEYC's online store features several guidance-related products for sale, including brochures, posters, books, training packs, and the DVD series *Facing the Challenge: Working with Children Who Use Challenging Behaviors* developed in cooperation with Video Active Productions and Devereux Center for Resilient Children. NAEYC offers technology-based learning, face-to-face training, an annual institute, and an annual conference.

Technical Assistance Center on Social Emotional Intervention for Young Children (TACSEI)

http://challengingbehavior.fmhi.usf.edu

Initially funded by the US Department of Education's Office of Special Education Programs, TACSEI offers many free online resources, including handouts, training materials, research summaries, "Teaching Tools for Young Children with Challenging Behavior," a program-wide positive behavior support booklet, and more. Many resources are based upon the Pyramid Model for Supporting Social and Emotional Competence in Infants and Young Children. Although the initial funding has ended, TACSEI resources are also available through the Pyramid Model Consortium at www.pyramidmodel.org.

Zero to Three: National Center for Infants, Toddlers and Families

www.zerotothree.org

Zero to Three provides free online resources about social and emotional development, temperament, early language literacy, and challenging behavior. The sections for professionals and parents are both very useful. Products are also available for sale. Zero to Three offers an annual conference and other training through a variety of funded projects.

Resources from Redleaf Press

For more information on these products, visit Redleaf Press's website at www.redleafpress.org.

Bilmes, Jenna. 2012. *Beyond Behavior Management: The Six Life Skills Children Need*. 2nd ed.

Hewitt, Deborah. 2011. *So This Is Normal Too?* 2nd ed.

Jacobson, Tamar. 2008. *"Don't Get So Upset!" Help Young Children Manage Their Feelings by Understanding Your Own*.

Langworthy, Sara E. 2015. *Bridging the Relationship Gap: Connecting with Children Facing Adversity*.

Oehlberg, Barbara. 2014. *Making It Better: Activities for Children Living in a Stressful World.* 2nd ed.

Puckett, Margaret B., Janet K. Black, and Joseph M. Moriarity. 2007. *Understanding Infant Development.*

Puckett, Margaret B., Janet K. Black, and Joseph M. Moriarity. 2007. *Understanding Preschooler Development.*

Puckett, Margaret B., Janet K. Black, and Joseph M. Moriarity. 2007. *Understanding Toddler Development.*

Riley, Dave, Robert R. San Juan, Joan Klinkner, and Ann Ramminger. 2008. *Social and Emotional Development: Connecting Science and Practice in Early Childhood Settings.*

Saifer, Steffen. 2017. *Practical Solutions to Practically Every Problem: The Survival Guide for Early Childhood Professionals.* 3rd ed.

Schweikert, Gigi, Jeniece Decker, and Jennifer Romanoff. 2017. *Winning Ways: Supporting Positive Behavior.*

Schweikert, Gigi, Jeniece Decker, and Jennifer Romanoff. 2017. *Winning Ways: Responding to Behavior.*

Schweikert, Gigi, Jeniece Decker, and Jennifer Romanoff. 2017. *Winning Ways: Guiding Challenging Behavior.*

Smith, Connie Jo, Charlotte M. Hendricks, and Becky S. Bennett. 2014. *Growing, Growing Strong 1: Body Care.*

Smith, Connie Jo, Charlotte M. Hendricks, and Becky S. Bennett. 2014. *Growing, Growing Strong 2: Fitness and Nutrition.*

Smith, Connie Jo, Charlotte M. Hendricks, and Becky S. Bennett. 2014. *Growing, Growing Strong 3: Safety.*

Smith, Connie Jo, Charlotte M. Hendricks, and Becky S. Bennett. 2014. *Growing, Growing Strong 4: Social and Emotional Well-Being.*

Smith, Connie Jo, Charlotte M. Hendricks, and Becky S. Bennett. 2014. *Growing, Growing Strong 5: Community and Environment.*